I0493027

Climb to the Top

A Guide to Unleash
the Power of Your Inner Entrepreneur

By: Curt Hinson

Climb to the top by Curt Hinson

© 2016 by Curt Hinson. All rights reserved.
No part of this book may be reproduced in any
written, electronic, recording, or photocopying
form without written permission of the author,
Curt Hinson.
Cover Design by: Curt Hinson
Editing by: Curt Hinson
Hinson, Curt, 1984 – Climb to the top

1. Entrepreneurship 2. Motivation
First Edition

Table of Contents

Introduction

Chances are, if you're reading this book, it's because you want to do something different than the norms of society (working a "real job") or you need to re-ignite your entrepreneurial fire, that will allow you to grow not only your business, but as a person also. For those of you wanting to do something different, maybe you do not know how or where to get started. Perhaps you've received incorrect information and bought into the myth that you need an excessive amount of money that you do not have, to get started. Maybe you've tried a few things and nothing has really worked, and you're still looking for answers to guide you to a successful path. Maybe you've been somewhat successful as an entrepreneur, but need and want to take your pursuit to a higher level. Perhaps you're a parent, mentor, or leader who is looking for reading material for someone under your wing that needs additional guidance. Do any of these resonate with you?

I believe every person has the potential to be an entrepreneur in one way or the other. I also believe there is nothing wrong with the 9 to 5, but for most working for yourself and by your own terms, is far more appealing.

There are a number of topics that will be covered as well as stories of successful entrepreneurs, some known, and some not as well known. These people were not born into wealth, and their success was not given to them. Most of these people are no different than you or I. The exception is their mindset, which we will also discuss in this book.

Regardless where you are in your life journey, just starting out, already on the pavement towards success, or mentoring someone; there is something for everyone in this book who wants to unleash their potential or to help others unleash theirs. You will find in this book some of the secrets that are not really that secret to success. If you find yourself where I was when I was 18, of wanting to, thinking about, but having no idea how to get started, this book is for you. This book is also for you if you are the parent or mentor of that 18-year-old or 30-year-old still pursuing one entrepreneurial venture after the other.

So I have to ask you these series of questions. What are you doing currently? What do you want to do? Are you happy with how things are going right now in your life? What are your aspirations? Where do you see yourself in a month, six months, a year, five years, ten years from now?

Take a pen and notebook and write those questions down. Answer honestly and those questions will be visited again later in this book. In order to fully understand and receive the information you're about to receive; you must have an open mind. You must also eliminate, or at least tune out, any self-defeating mindset, and preconceived notions about being an entrepreneur.

Whether we admit it or not, we all dream about a better life in one way or another. There is never a right or wrong dream, as each of us are unique in our own way; therefore, our dreams are unique to each of us. Some of us have long ago given up on those dreams, or don't even dare to allow them to surface for one reason or another. We will touch upon that as well in this book. Before diving into the first chapter I will kick it off with this quote.

"If you have a dream, you can spend a lifetime studying, planning, and getting ready for it. What you should be doing is getting started." Drew Houston

The seeds we sow today will be ready for harvest before we know it. The longer you wait to plant, the longer you have to wait to yield results.

If you are procrastinating and done little to nothing, use this as your kick in the pants to getting started. If you're chasing the next entrepreneurial chicken pursuit, even better. For those of you who have already taken action, you're already ahead in the game.

There are times when the pursuit seems like chasing a chicken, your goals always ahead of you no matter how fast you run. It zigs and zags, clucks about, and you want to give up. What you expect to be easy ends up being far more of a challenge than you expect, however, in the end the pursuit will pay off if you keep at it.

Allow this book to be your starter guide, or the spark you need to continue moving forward. Success is attainable, but only if you're willing to put in the time, effort, and hard work. This leads us to chapter one, and answers the question; What is an entrepreneur?

Chapter 1

What is an Entrepreneur?

Many of you have heard this word; some know there is a magazine by the same name. So what or who is an entrepreneur? What do they do? How do they make their money? How do I myself become one?

"Entrepreneurs are willing to work 80 hours a week to avoid working 40 hours a week." — Lori Greiner

Some of you may already be turned off by this quote, and there's a reason for it which we will discuss later in the book. Think about it; would you be willing to work 50, 60, 70, 80, or more hours a week as an entrepreneur or 40 hours a week for someone else?

For most entrepreneurs, it's not about the money; it's not about how many hours worked. These people are more concerned about having the freedom to do business their way, on their terms, and by the schedule they set. Now this may not be all of the motivating factors, and I may be just scratching the surface. My point is the entrepreneur is not someone that has some special powers that you don't have. These people are no different than you, and their "secrets to success" aren't really that secret. You can easily find them and apply those principles into your life.

Everyone has their definition of an entrepreneur. Some envision people such as Steve Jobs, Bill Gates, or Warren Buffett as entrepreneurs. Others may vision someone opening a small business in a local community. Honestly, there is no right or wrong answer, and with the right mindset, you too could be an entrepreneur yourself. The world is filled with entrepreneurs, from the kid with a lemonade stand, to the successful real estate mogul, and everywhere in-between. These people are not only dreamers, but also doers; movers and shakers. They are willing to take risks, work the long hours, and push forward despite the obstacles. These individuals have made the decision to live their life, to work by their terms, and not by the terms set out by anyone else.

Entrepreneurs have their eyes set on a vision of what they want to accomplish. What sets these people apart from the others is their focus, tenacity, ability to adapt, and overcome the obstacles that come their way. They see an opportunity where others may not, and are not swayed when others do not see or understand their vision. Despite skepticism from others, they push forward, even if the odds are not in their favor.

Many entrepreneurs share many common characteristics, however, not all share the same the same traits There really is no map set out to say that in order to be an entrepreneur, you must do this, that, and the other or possess certain a list of traits otherwise you won't be successful. So if you find that the characteristics of someone like Warren Buffet is not aligned with how you are; don't think that you've already lost the battle because you're not exactly like him, or have the self-defeating mindset of that you're not good enough to even try to be an entrepreneur.

Every entrepreneur is unique in their own way and offer a vision and talents to the world. These people are honestly no different than you. We will discuss some of the habits and actions that need to be taken to align you closer to the entrepreneurial mindset and away from the employee mindset. We'll discuss the employee mindset later on.

Entrepreneurs have a vision and passion that gets them excited to wake up in the morning, work long hours, and give their best; day in and day out. Though for some, the long hours and such is far too much in some people's opinion. Entrepreneurs are a special group of people and anyone is welcome to join the club. The secret is getting started and to continue pushing forward despite any obstacles.

Chapter 2

People are funny creatures

"When dealing with people, remember you are not dealing with creatures of logic, but creatures of emotion." Dale Carnegie – American writer, lecturer, developer of self-improvement, salesmanship, corporate training, public speaking and interpersonal skills.

No matter where you are in life, what job function you have in your career, if you work for yourself, and so on, there will be people. You are going to have to deal with people in one way or another. Unless you decide to live in the wilderness alone and to live off the land, there will always be the need to interact with those funny creatures called people.

In order to be successful in any industry and life in general, you have to learn how to deal with others. Yes, I know people can be difficult, they do dumb things, and they think asinine thoughts. With that being said, however, no matter how dumb, petty, or stupid others may seem to be, someone very well think the same thing about you.

The people that annoy you the most could be someone that another person is hanging on their every word and cannot get enough of listening to them and their stories. I've found those who annoy you the most there is some reason for it. Either they have glaring traits that you too, hold as well, yet you find this person's traits to be more profound, or you've found yourself creating an energy about yourself that you basically "hate everyone." Hate may be a strong word, but how many of us have said it, or heard friends and family be loud and proud about hating people?

I think one thing I had to learn quickly is that you have to find a way to deal with a vast variety of personalities. I have dealt with people from just about every walk of life throughout my career. There are so many things to be learned from others, even if it is a reminder not to find yourself engaging in the poor habits they may have, and make a point not to allow their mediocrity to become yours. If misery loves company, so does mediocrity.

As humans, being the funny people we are, will say and do so many things that may mean well but can have negative impacts on those around us. Out of fear we will tell our friends or loved ones not to take that new job, or start that business because "the economy is bad," or "there are way too many people trying to become singers, actors, writers, and it's just a tough industry. You better stick to going to college and getting that office job." Then we will pat ourselves on the back for making our friend or loved one face reality and keeping them from making a huge mistake in life. Now by saying these things, have we really done that person any good? Have we done ourselves any good by attempting to hinder that person to shoot for the stars?

Here is a little experiment, post on your social media account "I got the job!" And see what your response is. A week or so later post "I just started my own business!" And see what sort of response is compared to your first post.

I could almost guarantee that you will get more "likes" and comments by claiming you got the new job versus doing something daring like deciding to be your own boss. Plus, if you really do post "I got the job" this week and "I started my own business" next week, your friends and family will probably question your mental stability. Yet all we do is roll our eyes at the friend who met the love of their life for the third time this year and it's only April. Know what I am saying?

Now look there is nothing wrong with working a 9 to 5, nor is there anything wrong with owning your own business. Both are highly respectable regardless of what others may say or think. I don't know why as Americans many have grown more accustomed to just do the 9 to 5 versus trying to own their own business. It can be scary, it can be unpredictable, however, you'll never know unless you go for it.

Your decision to be where you are in life is not the same decision for someone else, regardless of how close they are to you. If you're a pilot and your son or daughter dreams of doing something outside of the airline industry, that is their decision. Though it would be wonderful for them to follow in your footsteps, you have to remember you can't make their decisions for them. What you can do, however, is encourage them, despite the fact they may not want to follow in your footsteps. This world would be an incredibly different place if we encouraged each other to follow our calling versus trying to fit them into a mold that they very well may not fit in.

What people fail to realize is that there are unlimited resources and wealth to be earned if you work for it, and eliminate your mental barriers. Am I starting to sound like every other book you've read? News flash it's true!

Truth be told there is nothing new under the sun when it relates to any topic, how to grow a garden, how to make killer sales, how to get closer to God, how to become a better person, and the list can be infinite. The difference is your mindset and openness to change.

Have you ever heard the saying "good things come to those who wait?" I'm going to tell you that it is a complete truck load of rubbish. Good things come from those who hustle and have the right mindset and attitude. You can change the world around you by just adjusting your poor attitude.

Don't get me wrong here, there are some times you do have to sit back and let certain things come to you, especially when you find yourself pursuing something that continually seems to be 5 steps ahead and you can never quite catch up to. It really is a matter of practicing successful habits, eliminating a great deal of our mental junk food, and staying focused.

What I mean by waiting for something to come to you is that you've done your part, you've sharpened your ax and chopped away, yet the tree won't fall despite your best efforts. Then the wind starts to blow, and your tree finally falls to the ground. What I am not saying is sitting next to the tree (the tree being in this case, whatever your dream or pursuit is) and do absolutely nothing expecting that tree to magically fall.

Another example would be bird watching, you know all your birds, have your birdwatchers book, and binoculars. If you put out food and run around trying to catch the attention of those lovely fowl, you'll do nothing but scare them off. If you put the food out and sit still at a safe distance, you'll find a variety of birds make their way to your bird seed.

Point is good things do come to those who do the work, not those that sit around hoping it happens, or wishing it, but refuse to actually put forth any effort.

The saying "attitude is everything" is pretty much spot on. You could view the world as a bright and beautiful place, while someone else experiencing the same thing you are, may view the world as dark, evil, and a sad place to call home for the human race. It all depends on the person. It could be a beautiful summer morning, the most beautiful morning you've ever witnessed, and someone could have something terrible to say about it. "It's too humid, I hate the summer, I wish it were the fall."

Often times, many of us find the attitudes of others becoming our attitude as well, except the ones that are upbeat and pleasant, we just think those people are on something or fake. Am I right?

We humans are flawed by nature, so don't beat yourself (or anyone else) up for not being perfect. We all do dumb things, make mistakes, fail, give up, and so on. If you find yourself in need of making some changes in your life, you're in good company. I understand the struggles and woes that many of us face on a daily basis. The difference is learning how to deal with what life throws your way.

Chapter 3

Risk

"Security is mostly superstition. It does not exist in nature, nor do the children of men as a whole experience it. Avoiding danger is no safer in the long run than outright exposure. Life is either a daring adventure or nothing." -Helen Keller

One thing that holds many people back from becoming an entrepreneur is that they find it to be risky. There are a lot of things that will be risky starting out and along the way. We run the risk of being ill-prepared, negative feedback from others and a negative impact on our finances.

With risk also comes reward. Many accept security of a steady paycheck. For some the thought of freedom from the 9 to 5 motivates them more than the so called security of that steady job. I can tell you first hand, for the longest time I was more motivated by having a check every two weeks versus the freedom working for myself would allow. As I got older, I learned new skills, and learned valuable life lessons. I then became more inclined to break away from the regular job world to a life that harbored the freedom I desired.

No longer was the thought process of the employee mindset, keeping me running around in the same circle. The 40-hour work week on someone else's terms became far less appealing. Why wouldn't someone be willing to do the work now, even if it requires more hours in the beginning? It may be scary, it may be tiring, but in the end your efforts will be worth it.

I honestly admire people who start off with the entrepreneurial spirit, and do not get addicted to the steady paycheck. There are many people like my brother who has never had a true steady 9 to 5 type job. He's always had to hustle in one way or another to make a dollar. To him, and many like him, the risk of not taking action far outweighed the risk of taking action.

When you really look at it, risk isn't the issue. It's the fear of the unknown. Out of fear you refuse to take action because you have thoughts of "If you start your own business how and when will you get paid? Who will be your clients? How will you attract them? What if things don't go as planned?" Don't allow the risk factor to hold you back. If allowed, risk, and the fear of it can be paralyzing.

So let's say you decide to take the road of the steady paycheck. What happens if the job you thought was secure lays off your department? What if the company folds? What if the economy takes a turn for the worst and your pay and/or hours are cut? You see, there is risk in having a job just as there is in being an entrepreneur.

Starting out you may have to spend some of or the majority of your own funds. You may do well, but you also risk losing some or all of it. There are numerous stories out there of entrepreneurs risking everything they had, that have laid their fortunes on the line and lost it all.

Now I mean none of this to scare you or to convince you not to pursue your dreams and goals. What I want to drill in is the fact that you will have to hustle and there will always be risk in anything you choose to do in life.

It's your responsibility to learn how to take those chances without allowing the fear of the unknown paralyze you. With great risk can come great reward or a great learning opportunity. Note I did not say risk can present great failure. I say this because failure is what it is, a learning opportunity. We will talk more about failure later in the book.

For now, keep this in mind; risk taking is an essential part of being a human being. We must take risks to get to where we want to be in life and in order to succeed. There is always going to be uncertainty, but we must be brave enough to walk down the path of uncertainty. With experience comes the resourcefulness to reduce risk because you have the wisdom to know what did and did not work in past experiences.

You cannot expect to do great things if you are not willing to accept the fact there will be risks, and be willing to step outside of your comfort zone to go after your desires. In order to get different results, you must do things differently.

This all being said about risk leads me to the next chapter. The employee mindset.

Chapter 4

Employee Mindset

I must provide you with a sarcasm warning for the following chapter. Although there is a bit of sarcasm, there is a little truth tied to what you're about to read. Some of what you will read in this chapter has been taken from some of my former thoughts and beliefs, as well as those of others that I've encountered in my life journey. As you read this, take a moment to think if any of this is relatable to you or others around you.

One of the biggest challenges starting out as an entrepreneur is having the employee mindset. With the employee mindset most of us are conditioned to accept the safety of having a steady paycheck versus the possibility of little to no payoff by doing something on our own. Owning your own business is something most consider outside of what's normal. People who own, or aspire to own their own business are viewed with a scoff and a head tilt. Because, you know, "that's stupid; everyone knows in order to really make money you have to have a real job."

Having a "real job" in a sense is pretty much like jail. The exception being you go home at the end of the day. It's totally "normal" to give 40 hours per week (or more) to someone else. You give them 40 hours, and in return they give you a check. They tell you what to do, when to do it, and how to do it. You're told how to dress, and on rare special occasions, or if you give them some of your hard earned money, you can wear jeans. You're told when to show up, when to go to lunch, and when to go home. They dictate how much money you make. If you don't think it's enough, you can either quit, or complain and risk getting fired, because let's face it; you're totally replaceable, and probably by someone who would work for much less than you're being paid. Does this sound like freedom to you?

As an employee most give 100% each week:
10% on Monday (Because let's face it, Monday's suck right?)
25% on Tuesday (A little extra motivation since Monday is now in the past.)
30% on Wednesday (Halfway through the week, so we can afford to give a little extra)
25% on Thursday (Slipping down a tad on our productivity, but still doing better than Monday.)
10% on Friday (The weekend is almost here,

honestly no one can expect much on Friday right?)

The above formula is adjusted slightly if you plan on taking off one of those days, or the following week. Maybe the beginning of your week isn't Monday, but you get the point. Some of you may be thinking "Well, I give way more than that." Okay so be it. Regardless, do you honestly believe that this life was meant to spend your best years fulfilling someone else's dream?

It's very unfortunate that we are conditioned from an early age to go to school, then college, get a job, work there for 30, 40, or 50 years, save up a little money during that time, and hopefully retire comfortably. If we're really lucky the company, we retire from will give us a gold watch upon our exit.

"The three most harmful addictions are heroin, carbohydrates, and a monthly salary." Nassim Nicholas Taleb

Now look, I'm not anti-business, I'm not anti-college, nor am I anti-job. I just hold a firm belief that being an entrepreneur grants each person more freedom than a "normal" 9 to 5.

The time we live in is changing rapidly. The world is changing. The economy is changing. How we do business is changing. Since the great recession, companies have been doing more with less. It's an employer's market when it comes to seeking out new talent. On average for every one job available, an employer receives around 250 resumes. Of those resumes received, only about 2% will actually receive an interview. In many cases when a person leaves a position by either his or her decision or by force; the position is merged into someone else's job duties. Technology is now a big player in either replacing, and/or eliminating the need for a warm body to provide a service or do a task. Take the banking industry or retail for instance, thanks to technology; there is very little reason why anyone would need to go into a brick and mortar location to do anything.

The idea of working for one's self, being an entrepreneur, being your own boss, freelancing, or whatever else you want to call it, is becoming not only more and more appealing but a necessity given the changes in the world around us.

Nowadays all you need is a cell phone, laptop, and an internet connection to do business. The possibilities to make new contacts and ways do business is almost infinite. People have made it big in network marketing by utilizing the power of the internet, or got their book published by using the online resources to self-publish, or became famous by posting their home videos online.

This isn't the same world we lived in when I was a teenager. This isn't the same world as it was when I graduated college. I could go on for days talking about how things are different now than in the past, or show you so many examples of how people have made money online or other methods. The issue at hand is, however, unless you disconnect from the status quo that is, the employee mindset, you will never reach your full potential.

If someone paying you $7.25, $10.00, $15.00, or $20.00, per hour for you to sell them an hour of your time you will never get back is appealing to you, by all means continue doing so. This being taken into consideration, though, keep in mind, it is not your employer's responsibility to keep you as an employee, to make your life better, or make your dreams come true. They made an agreement that if you work an hour with them, they will pay you a set amount for that hour and each hour after that you do some form of work for them. All said, you trade your time for money. Where is the freedom in that?

Chapter 5

Ignore the naysayers

"When everything seems to be against you, remember that the airplane takes off against the wind, not with it." Henry Ford

It doesn't matter what you choose to pursue; there will always be naysayers. These people are more often than not, always negative and pessimistic. Instead of saying "it can be done," instead always say "it can't be done."

One should always expect some form of resistance, and should never be surprised when it comes your way. Keep your eyes on your vision and push forward.

These people could very well be those that are close to you, such as friends and family. We often seek the approval of others, especially the ones that are closest to us. So when you share an idea with one of these people, there is a good chance their reaction will have a great deal of influence if you push forward or drop the idea altogether.

I totally get it. You want mom, dad, your mammaw, or your best friend to be gung-ho about your new business. When some, if not all of those people have little good to say in response, it can be terrible. I'm thankful I never experienced the naysayers with my own immediate family, however, I know that is not always the case for everyone. I will say though, there are those in my life who I've made a conscious decision to share very little with them when it comes to my dreams, goals, and desires. I already know what they are going to say, or not say. So why bother tossing the ball their way when I know I won't receive a positive return?

Another naysayer could be yourself. You know, that voice, that string of thoughts deep down that tell you "I can't do that! I'm not smart enough! I don't know anything about doing x, y, or z." Honestly, this is another one of those lists that could be endless if you wanted to focus on all the negatives. To move forward you must stop your self-doubting beliefs, and replace them with a positive voice.

There will be a level of risk in everything you do. One risk may be severing ties or at least limiting your contact with those who may be your biggest naysayers.

When Dolly Parton wanted to buy into the theme park now known as Dollywood, many of her advisors and members of her team told her it was an unwise decision. (Those naysayers no longer work for her.) Dolly had the vision early on to create jobs and provide stability in the area near where she grew up. Though she had no theme park experience, she surrounded herself with those who were experts in that area. Despite the naysayers, well, we all know how successful Dollywood has become.

If Dolly had succumbed to the naysayers within, or externally, we may have never known the goodness of the fantastic theme park in the Great Smokey Mountains.

Is there something you've thought of, or pursued only to get resistance? How did you handle it?

If you have your vision, your dream, stop at nothing and make it a reality. Surround yourself with positive influence, those who are on a similar journey, or who are a few steps ahead.

Learn from their success, and how they dealt with the negative vibes that their naysayers through their way.

Chapter 6

Enough with the excuses already

"Excuses are the nails used to build the house of failure." - Unknown

We all have excuses to deal with our day to day lives. We use them to justify why we do or do not do things we should in our lives. We use excuses to justify poor habits, behaviors, and actions. It's no different with being an entrepreneur. There is always some sort of excuse that many of us use to justify why we don't pursue something outside of the 9 to 5 life. An excuse is a crutch, it is not noble, and it is not something that successful people use.

Here are a few excuses that are pretty typical.

These common excuses include but are not limited to:

It's not the right time.

"Don't wait. The time will never be just right." – *Napoleon Hill*

Many times people use the crutch phrase of "it's not the right time." "I will start a business when the time is right," etc. Basically, waiting for the right time is what most think of as a clever excuse to procrastinate in pursuing something outside of their comfort zone. If you wait for that perfect time, you may find yourself unable to ever find it. You'll wake up one day to realize all the time you squandered waiting, versus taking action. The seeds you sow today; you will reap in your future. By waiting to sow your seeds, you've only postponed reaping the fruits of your efforts. So by sowing nothing, you receive nothing in return.

So if today is not the right time, what makes you think tomorrow, next week, or when the economy gets better, or when we have a new president, that the perfect time will present itself to you? I can almost guarantee you that whatever excuse you have today, you will have tomorrow, next week, the next decade. The excuses may change to adjust to that point in your life. For example, "I'm too young," becomes "I'm too old." I don't know about you, but I'd much rather look back at my life and say "I can't believe I did that," versus "I wish I would have, or I regret I didn't take action then." Unless you have a sense of urgency to take action and make things happen, you'll make little to no progress in your entrepreneurial endeavors. You must identify your "why" get yourself motivated, and get to work.

It's not the perfect time because you don't have the money? You can't get financing?
Ever notice how when you decide to take action on something you've been putting off either, things just seem to fall in place, or everything seems to be going against you? How many of us have had the thought process of when it's easy, it's meant to be, but if challenged it isn't meant to happen? I've said it once, I'll say it again, if it were easy everyone would be doing it.

Todd Graves, CEO and founder of Raising Canes, had an extreme uphill battle when it came to opening his fast food restaurant that serves chicken finger meals only. The odds were not in his favor. Mr. Graves received the lowest grade in his class when he wrote a report outlining his fast food concept. Financing his venture was another hurdle. If he could get a banker to even meet with him, despite his business plan, would get shot down. Mr. Graves was even told by some, to give up and get a "real job."

Even though the odds were against him, Mr. Graves set out to raise his own capital to make his dream a reality. He didn't use crowd funding, he went to California to work as a boilermaker, and to Alaska as a salmon fisherman. He did this to raise the capital needed, even though, according to our conventional wisdom, he should have given up ten times over.

Needless to say, the first location of Raising Canes was eventually opened right outside the gates of Louisiana State University. This new restaurant was and is a hit. Raising Canes has expanded to over 250 locations.

The timing is never going to be perfect no matter the situation, your financial situation, the state of the economy, ect. If the timing isn't right in your opinion, that is merely an excuse for you not to have to take action and get started already.

It's too hard

"Nobody ever said being an entrepreneur was easy. I've had a lot of sleepless nights. Still do. But the freedom in my life makes it worth it." Tai Lopez

You're correct. It's not easy starting a business. Let's be even more honest, it may be the hardest thing you'll ever do. If you are someone that loves sleep, peace, and tranquility; you're going to risk losing some of that for a while. Sleep? You're going to lose lots of it. Peace with your mate? You're probably going to have a few battles with them. You will probably spend and possibly lose a good deal of your hard earned money. Scared yet? Or possibly am I just affirming your excuse? No one, not even me, said this entrepreneurial pursuit would be easy. If it were easy, everyone would be doing it.

My first entrepreneurial venture was being a realtor. I tell you right there, I had no idea how difficult it would be to get started. I gave it close to a year with very little luck. Then I gave up. Do you want to know why I had very little luck? I was getting out of it what I was putting into it, practically nothing. If you think taking only one day to put a few signs out around town, hand out a few business cards, or opening a webpage is all you have to do, you're wrong. That's the starting point.

Chances are whatever you decide to do, someone else is doing it too. You're going to have to expand your network beyond your friends, family, and co-workers. It won't always be easy, but if you work hard now, the payoff could be greater than you expected.

So many people want instant results. I've also found myself in the past wanting microwaveable instant results. Sure, I'd love to make a few million by the end of the year. I'd love to sell a million copies of my books so I could help as many people as possible. When it comes to any pursuit, it takes time.

"It's so funny looking back, but my so-called overnight success actually took 15 years. I remember when I didn't have any money, and my only car was mom's Hyundai." Criss Angel

Most people give up quickly because they do not see results as soon as they get started. They give up when folks tell them they are crazy, when friends and family don't answer the phone, when new clients are seemingly few and far between, or when the amount of hustle you're comfortable with isn't yielding enough results.

No, it's not always easy. I'm sorry to say, but it is a reality. Gardening is a hobby I enjoy some seasons more than others. Trust me when I say that even in my most involved spring seasons, I could not survive on the yield of my harvest. Why you may ask? Well, quite simply, I have never planted enough to yield an off the grid sort of harvest for one, and two I usually don't put in the effort required to yield an abundance.

I also have a peach tree, an orange tree, two apple trees, and a plum tree. None of the harvests would sustain life, even if I wanted them to. Now, if I had an orchard or heck, even a more sizable garden than I do now I'd probably have enough to put away, sell, and give away. I would also be required to put more time, effort, and energy into having a larger garden. Something I'm not willing to give at this current time.

It's the same with your entrepreneurial pursuit. If you think a few months of what you call hustle, posting pictures on social media, and talking to just a couple of people are going to yield you results that are going to put you on Forbes Magazine; you're sadly mistaken.

Yes, it's not easy. Yes, it takes time, effort, and energy. Yes, it requires you to get out of your comfort zone. No, it will not be a cakewalk.

"Anyone who wants to sell you overnight success or wealth is not interested in your success; they are interested in your money." Bo Bennett

Now that we have touched on the difficulty excuse, we have to talk briefly about the snake oil salesperson. This is someone selling you the dream, and the easy money. All of this can be yours for little to no effort. Not true. They just want your money. They make their money by taking yours and giving you little in return.

Not everything is a scam, however, trust your instincts. If it's too good to be true, it probably is. Be more trusting of the person that tells you they are where they are because of hard work and that they built their empire over time. Be less trusting of the person or group promising wealth by just giving them hundreds, or thousands of dollars with the promise of easy results.

I'll give you a good example. I received an email that promised to change my life and make all of my financial dreams come true. I did not believe it, however, I figured I would look into whatever scam, it was they were trying to sell me. Upon clicking the link, there were numerous testimonials of "everyday people" just like you and I, that had $50 in the bank, and now all of a sudden by using this program that didn't require them to do anything, were now making $5,000 - $8,000 per month, and some earning even more than that.

Oh wow, that's cool, ain't that something? Well, it was obviously a scam and I will tell you why. First of all, one of the testimonials the person claimed they had $67 in their checking account, and always begging and borrowing money from people to pay their bills. Now that this person signed up for the get rich program she doesn't worry about money any more.

Wow! What a compelling story. So I go further on the page to sign up. They want $500 to get started. So, where did these people with nothing in their checking accounts get the $500 to sign up? No one's testimonial, that claimed they didn't have any money in the first place, explained how they paid the sign-up fee. If you, honestly and truly do not have $500 to blow, but find some way to get the money and give it away, what do you think the end result will be?

Have you heard anything such as:

"Yeah your life sucks, so did mine. You need to make more money, so did I. Now give me money you don't have so you will be able to make money and be rich like I am."

Some of you may equate that to network marketing, and other things that you've been either been arm wrestled into, or know someone who has. Now I'm not saying network marketing is a scam, however, there are some people that are more concerned with making their own dollar than they are in helping you get yours as well. This is something you're going to have to trust your instincts with. Honestly, you need to trust your instincts when any opportunity that comes your way, or what seems like an opportunity. You've got to make the decision if it is right for you.

Again, I'm not knocking network marketing. I know many people have made it big in that industry, however, they didn't make it big by just buying a $1,000 kit and then all the riches came to them easy breezy. They had to work, and had to work hard. If someone tries to sell it to you as the easiest thing you will ever do, or something like that, they are probably lying.

Again to be successful takes time, effort, and energy. It's not limited to just those three things either. If you keep at it, and make it into an overnight success, for you it will not be so overnight even though it will seem that way to some. When people see that you went from driving a 20-year-old clunker to driving a $100,000 car, they might consider that your overnight success story. Let that be your opportunity to mentor the willing. Share your journey, share what worked, what didn't, and then help them become their best.

People don't really think of me as an entrepreneur. Heck, I really don't see myself as one either.

So no one sees you as an entrepreneur? Why do you think that is? Could it be that these people that claim you're not cut out for it, or some other lame reason; could actually fall into the naysayer category? So who doesn't think it's a good fit for you? Is it friends, family, or co-workers?

As you sprout your entrepreneurial endeavors, you're going to have to ignore the cynics and naysayers. Make a point to stay away from them as much as possible. Be that as it may, if you take the jump and begin your business, you will be shocked at how quick individuals who were initially naysayers will consider you to be some sort of business genius once you make it big. Discernment is reality, and when you are the one that is in charge, you will be seen as a pioneer regardless of the way that you used to be. It doesn't matter if you were a client administration director, a finance agent, or a janitor. Individuals regard the people who have taken a risk and put their notoriety, money, and vocation at stake.

You can try once, try again, try a million times and face setbacks and disappointments. This does not mean you're not an entrepreneur, or that you're a bad entrepreneur. The same people that think you're a failure, not cut out for it, or that you should just get a real job, will consider you a genius when your pursuit finally takes off and you're on your way to the top. Kind of like how people that hated you in high school want to be your best friend once you get famous, and they tell everyone how the two of you met, ect. The same concept applies when you finally find something that works for you and starts taking off.

If you don't see yourself as an entrepreneur; why is this? Could it be your own self-doubt? Could it be you already bought into the myths of the world about going to school and getting a "real job?" Could it be fear that is driving you to stay within the bounds of your comfort zone? Could it be a combination of a few or all of the above?

The word entrepreneur to some may be the 'shark' types on television. You know the successful ones. We snicker at the guy or gal that's working two jobs and trying to get an entrepreneurial pursuit off the ground. Come on, be honest. You know you've had some sort of nasty conversation with someone about a friend or loved one who is trying their darndest to do something outside of the pre-conceived norm. Now that it's your turn you certainly don't want people to know, especially those who you had those gossip sessions with.

Perhaps it's just that the fear of working too much, and/or not having steady income just paralyzes you to the point you do nothing but procrastinate. Maybe you are just procrastinating because procrastinating is what you do best?

I've said it once, I'll say it again, and probably will say a million more times while I'm here on earth; if you want life to be different, you, Y O U, must do things differently in order to make different and better things happen in your life.

If you're at a point that you want to do something different, but do not know where to start, there is ample information out there to get the idea wheels a turning in your mind.

I highly recommend reading books related to wealth building, as well as other self-help reading materials that will assist you in becoming a better version of yourself

Remember, to align yourself closer to being what your idea of an entrepreneur is; you're going to need to do things differently in your life. Although at first reading, meditation, or anything else along those lines may be uncomfortable. I will tell you that once I got comfortable doing these things, I've found some of my most creative ideas come to me during or not long after meditation, reading, listening to an audio book, or doing something else that allows me to think and expand my mind.

Another thing to remember also, unless you make the decision, you won't do much of anything. It's one thing to talk about it, pray about it, or kind of half way start something. It's another thing if you have a hell bound determination that you will conquer, do things differently, and make opportunities happen. You can want to want to do something, but wanting to and deciding to are two completely different animals. So what's your decision? Are you going to allow things to stay the way they are currently, or, are you going to make the decision to get your pursuit started and off the ground?

I need to go to college

What does Michael Dell, Steve Jobs, Bill Gates, Mark Zuckerberg, and Travis Kalanick have in common? Each are successful entrepreneurs, and each of them dropped out of college.

"You don't have to be a genius or a visionary or even a college graduate to be successful. You just need a framework and a dream." Michael Dell

Now, what does Bob Proctor, Andrew Carnegie, Coco Chanel, David Green, Ray Kroc, Henry Ford, and Richard Branson have in common? They did not go to college at all. Ray Kroc, Richard Branson, and Henry Ford dropped out of high school. So there you have it. The argument that a high school education plus a college degree is required to succeed is invalid. Neither of those pieces of paper will make you a better person or a better entrepreneur.

Another example is Tai Lopez. He is a successful entrepreneur and mentor. As an avid reader, Tai has read over 5,000 books. He successfully climbed his way out of sleeping on a sofa in a mobile home to living comfortably in southern California. Before age 30 he became a self-made millionaire. Guess what? He didn't go to college yet has been able to achieve the good life.

You've got to do what is right for you, not what was right for someone else, even if you hear "you don't want to be a loser like me so you better go to college."

The average college debt is around $30,000. Note, that this is the average. There are plenty of students and former students whose debt number is far higher than the $30,000 mark. We graduate high school with zero debt, and graduate college deeply in debt. Regardless if we spend $10,000, $50,000, or $100,000 on our college education, there is no real guarantee we will get a job.

There are numerous people with degrees that allow them to do nothing more than they are already doing, still waiting tables, and working in coffee shops. Don't let the advertisements on television fool you. Those people are paid actors.

So if you think that giving $500 or $1,000 to start a "business" in network marketing is a scam, then why in the hell would you spend $30,000 or more at a college or university in hopes that your degree will make your life better and easier?

Now don't get me wrong. If your passion is to

practice law, medicine, build bridges, or any other field that requires higher learning I say go for it. If you don't know what you want to do yet, or have a young one who doesn't know yet what they want to do, it's probably best to figure out what it is that you want to do before you spend money you don't have to spend, and may never pay off.

All of this said, however, I am not anti-education, nor am I pro-drop out of high school. My point is there are numerous success stories where the people did not follow the norms of society and climbed their way to the top. If you're considering not going to college, or dropping out of college, or you've already finished college; the amount of hustle required to build a successful business is all the same, with or without a degree.

If your desire is to go to college for business, learn a trade, or what have you, go for it. I will say this, however, shop around and find the best price. Avoid proprietary (for profit) colleges and universities. Avoid them, avoid them, avoid them like the plague. These types of organizations have one thing at heart, their investors and shareholders, not their students. Not only will it be more expensive to go to their "college," when it comes time to graduate and get a job, most people won't even recognize the name. Trust me, I know, and there are countless others have figured this out the hard way as well.

The "advisors" at these institutions are nothing more than commissioned sales persons that are worried more about meeting their quota, than they are of figuring out if college is really a better option for you or not. Sure, you may be able to get your bachelors in half the time than a traditional university, but is the excessive cost really worth it? Now a days more and more traditional universities are offering blended or completely online degree options. So again if you have made the decision to go to university, shop around, and choose wisely.

You have the option to educate yourself far differently today than before the dawn of the internet age. We live in a day where the amount of information available to us for free, is almost infinite. If there is a topic you want to learn about you can easily find it online, and even take a class for free from leading universities across the globe. You can learn about anything you so desire with a google search, some time, and a little research. So before you spend money with a car-salesman type "university" or trade school; consider your options.

I believe often times people use the education

excuse as a crutch to keep from going after their entrepreneurial pursuit. Then by the time you graduate you're in so much debt you practically have no choice but to go get a real job. If you do choose to go to school, I would highly encourage you to pursue your entrepreneurial aspirations while you are in college. Don't wait for a new day, until you graduate, or whatever excuse you come up with. The longer you put things off, the more likely you will not get started in the first place. Don't allow learning more to become that excuse.

Successful people pursue a lifetime of learning, not just the specified times only during grade school then college. In your entrepreneurial pursuit, in order to climb to the top, you must commit to be in a state of constant learning. It doesn't matter if you're taking a course, reading a book, or a trade magazine. If you want to become the master of your craft, reading and learning more should be your priority. You will earn more as you learn more. Now that does not mean just because you read something you're going to make a fist wad of cash. Knowledge is only as powerful and lucrative as you make it to be. Unless you apply the new found knowledge, it will have little to no effect in your life, or your business.

If you want to climb to the top, lose the baggage that is your excuses

Lastly, if you really decide to climb your way to the top, come hell or high water, you will do whatever it takes. All of your excuses will not be relevant, nor will you allow them to cloud your dreams, vision, and pursuit. I'm sure you can find quite a few additional excuses. With what I have listed, and the ones that you are thinking of currently; what are you going to do starting right now to overcome your own excuses?

"When something is important enough, you do it even if the odds are not in your favor." – Elon Musk

Chapter 7

Courage

"Your time is limited, so don't waste it living someone else's life. Don't be trapped by dogma - which is living with the results of other people's thinking. Don't let the noise of others' opinions drown out your own inner voice. And most important, have the courage to follow your heart and intuition." – Steve Jobs

To be an entrepreneur, there is a level of courage that must be achieved in order to set things in motion. You will not only be facing your own fears, but the fears of others as well. The decision to live your life differently than the accepted "norm" will be a test of your character.

Regardless if your biggest obstacles are external or internal factors, you're going to have to face your fears and clearly understand your "why." Why do you want to be an entrepreneur? What factors are motivating you? There are a million reasons; well, honestly, a million excuses why not to be an entrepreneur. That being said, however, we can find a million reasons why we should be one.

Despite the state of the economy, who is in office, it seems the timing is not right, or other self-doubt issues; you must have the courage to start despite the obstacles. There are so many who have started out where you are right now, or even worse, and have been able to make a life for themselves far beyond anything they could have ever dreamed of.

Now by just being an entrepreneur does not guarantee you'll be an instant millionaire. You do have the opportunity, however, to start sowing the seeds that can lead you down the path of success.

It was once explained to me once, and took many years for it to make sense. You start out on a path in the woods. Before you know it, you find the beaten path you're supposed to be on. As you continue the path widens and becomes a dirt road. Keep moving forward and the dirt road becomes a gravel road, then an asphalt pavement, and before you know it you'll be on a concrete freeway to the top.

The only way to make this happen however, is to have the courage to get started, and go through the twists and turns. You must have the ability to bounce back after hitting a pothole, and remain focused on your goals. Sow the seeds of nothing and you will remain on the path to nowhere.

Courage along with determination helps you get started and also helps you to keep pushing forward when you fear that no one will buy your music, or buy your products, or offers you funding, and so on.

Courage is something you need when you face the group of naysayers that give every reason why you should not start your own business. You need it when the time comes to make those first few phone calls, speak to a group of people, or share your vision with your newly hired team.

"Courage is resistance to fear, mastery of fear-not absence of fear." Mark Twain

Let courage, drive you forward. Tap into it when fear, doubt, and naysayers stand in your way. It takes far more courage to pursue your dreams and goals than it does to sit on the sofa watching tv and playing video games. Actually, it takes zero courage to stay put in your comfort zone.

Chapter 8

Welcome to Discomfort; Your New Comfort Zone

"If you put yourself in a position where you have to stretch outside your comfort zone, then you are forced to expand your consciousness." Les Brown

To be a successful entrepreneur, you will have to do things that will make you quite uncomfortable. You will have to deal with friends, family, and coworkers that do not understand your vision, the discomfort of getting clients, or the discomfort of seeking out capital. This list could go on for days for the potential things that will take you out of your comfort zone.

If you remain in your comfort zone, your results may not be as great as you might expect. Regardless of what you may think, no one is going to be able to do this for you. You're going to have to do things differently in order to make a change in your life, business, finances, and so on.

You may have to make short term sacrifices in order to facilitate long term gain. One example would be taking a second job to pay off debt, or getting a not so great job, but pays awesome to help you build the capital you need to start your own business. Another thing that may be uncomfortable is taking the time out of your day to invest in yourself such as working out and/or studying about the venture you are starting.

Expecting different results for the same amount of time, effort, and energy you've been given is pretty much the definition of insanity. It's no different if you were to plant tomato seeds and then get upset when you don't grow a corn crop.

You will have to get uncomfortable, there is no reason to expect there not to be some degree of discomfort starting out.

Start off small by making small adjustments in your everyday life that are outside of your comfort zones.

Here are a few examples:

Take a different route to work

Try out a new restaurant (and don't search online reviews)

Make quicker decisions and trust your gut

Now this may not completely sound like such life altering adjustments to get you out of your comfort zone, however, if you're not willing to do the small things, you're not going to be willing to do things that will get you out of your comfort zone.

Look at it this way; if you're not willing to make a quick decision about shampoo instead of getting the same ole same ole and not take a long time trying to find an alternative, how are you going to handle quitting your day job when the time comes?

If you don't have the courage to do things differently, and get out of your comfort zone, you're going to risk a year from now, five years from now, a decade from now, being in the same place you are now, possibly a bit further, however, it will not be nearly as great as it could have been.

Take a few moments and write down the following:

1. Make a list of things that you consider part your comfort zone.
(An example would be your job, your daily and weekly routine, ect.)

2. How would you feel about quitting your job, prospecting, and working longer hours to achieve your goals? (Be honest here)

3. What easy adjustments could you make right now to prepare you for when the time comes to make even bigger decisions that may bring discomfort?

I listened to a guy speak at a seminar once who said that even though he was now in a place in life where he owned a pent house in Las Vegas, he was still uncomfortable. His reasoning was if you get too comfortable at any point in your life, you will stagnate and will not move forward. I know what you're thinking; "well if I owned a place in Las Vegas, that's a pretty good stopping point to be comfortable." I understand that point, however, I believe if you're willing to get comfortable once you reach a certain level, you will be willing to settle for far less. You'll start saying and thinking things such as "this ratty apartment is good enough," or "this junky car is good enough," or "I may as well get comfortable because I really don't think I can do any better than where I am right now." This list could go on for days with self-defeating thoughts that will keep one in their comfort zone. If you want to grow, if you want to do more and be more; you've got to step outside of your comfort zone. You must be comfortable being uncomfortable.

I will leave you with one more quote before closing out this chapter. Though there are numerous quotes related to this topic; I think this is one of my favorites.

"I don't like being stagnant. I want to continue to grow and just be better at what I do, and the only way to do that is to keep stepping outside of your comfort zone." Vanessa Hudgens

Chapter 9

Self-doubt

"Self-doubt kills talent." Edie McClurg

Self-doubt is nothing more than another manifestation of self-sabotaging behavior. One of the biggest battles you may have to fight is your own self-doubt. What I'm talking about are those thoughts of "What if I'm not good enough? What if I fail in this project? What if no one buys my book? What if no one wants to cast me for a role?"

At one point or another we've all faced a moment, or a period of self-doubt. There could be a number of reasons as to why you are currently or have previously dealt with self-doubt. The fear of the unknown, the naysayers in your life, could be motivating factors triggering your self-doubt. Past failures could play a significant role in the self-doubt that sets up shop in your mind, hindering you from moving forward in your pursuits.

Your success in your career or as an entrepreneur can be greatly affected by self-doubt. Your performance and motivation are diminished so therefore you do not step outside of your comfort zone. Self-doubt also triggers your self-defense mechanisms in an attempt to avoid failure. When you put all of this together, unfortunately you've inhibited your growth.

Overcoming self-doubt will not be easy for most people. In order to build your self-confidence and eliminate the self-doubt in your life that is holding you back, we've got to identify what those factors are, and find ways to rise above this self-sabotaging behavior.

The sad reality is, that we must be very mindful of the company we keep. If you are always broke, continuously hopping from one job you hate to another, and have a pessimistic view on life for example; chances are the five people you hang out with the most hold similar views and have the similar issues financially, mentally and spiritually.

I've watched a group of people start at broke, and remain there. I've also observed a group of people go from broke, then get a fire lit under their rear ends to make a change, and each of them elevate their status.

The difference between the first group and the second group is this; the first group found excuses as to why they were where they are. The second group took action and eliminated the self-doubt out of their life and come hell or high water, they decided to do whatever it takes to make a better life for themselves, and their family.

In order to grow and to unleash your inner power, you must become aware. Not only should you become aware of yourself and your thoughts; you must also become aware of your surroundings and the company that you keep.

If you are self-doubting due to fear of speaking in public, or because you don't know enough about a certain topic; work on those issues by consulting a coach or taking a class that will allow you to sharpen your skills and boost your confidence.

You also must stop seeking validation from others. If you're running with the crowd ate up with the employee mindset, their validation for you starting a new venture as an entrepreneur will not be encouraging. These people will validate all the reasons why you shouldn't do it. Which re-affirms all of your self-doubt in the first place.

One thing I found quite strange to practice, but now makes perfect sense to me is, not sharing my plans. By keeping my mouth shut, or by sharing with only a very select few people, I'm able to accomplish more as I work towards my goals. Reason for this is simply because if we share with too many people and they acknowledge it; your brain is tricked into thinking you have already accomplished the goal. You then run the risk of a self-doubt affirmation inadvertently making its way to the surface. "I never finish what I start. I'm all talk and no do."

Start feeding your mind with positive affirmations. One cannot move forward if they retain the same thoughts and habits that has kept them where they are currently. Now some may think that affirmations are cheesy or even ridiculous. You have the right to think and believe anything you want. I will tell you in my own life, and what I have observed in the life of others, those so called stupid and cheesy affirmations have made a difference. Give it a shot, what do you have to lose?

In your notebook, write the following questions down:

1. Write down a few of your self-doubts.
2. Why do you feel that way? What do you think caused you to believe these self-defeating affirmations?
3. On another sheet of paper, write down your self-doubts, then turn them into a positive.

Here are a couple of examples:

I'm not good enough.

I have the power within me to do things above and beyond my own expectations. I am on a journey to achieve greatness. I will do well. I am good enough.

I'm not cut out for this.

I only feel this way because I have not yet stepped outside of my comfort zone. I will strive to do my best, I will do my best. This is something I am cut out for and will do an excellent job at.

Spend a little bit of time with your self-doubt however, do not dwell on it, nor let it become a trigger to just wallow around in self-doubt and pity. Let me repeat that, do not let this become an activity that will allow you to wallow around in your pity and self-doubt. Do not write down "I'm not good enough" then say "You know what I'm right, I'm not good enough. I suck at everything I do. What was I thinking by even wanting to do something new, exciting, or different? I'm just going to fail anyway, so why bother?"

Focus more on the positives, be excited about the positive changes you are going to manifest into your life as you climb your way to the top!

Chapter 10

Remain Focused on Your Goals

"Successful people maintain a positive focus in life, no matter what is going on around them. They stay focused on their past successes rather than their past failures, and on the next action steps they need to take to get them closer to the fulfillment of their goals rather than all the other distractions that life presents to them." Jack Canfield

The path to success takes focus, even when things don't go the way you expect. There is so much out there that can distract us from maintaining our focus on our goals. Technology, social media, poor habits, etc. can be a hindrance to remaining focused.

We now live in a microwave type society. We want everything in an instant, and consider it a failure when results aren't delivered immediately. Most of us view success as a straight, upward path, from start to finish. The path to success is actually filled with ups, downs, twists, and turns.

In whatever your pursuit is, despite the twists and turns that will come your way, always remain focused on your goals and vision.

To remain focused, sort out your goals, and break them down into segments. An example would be goals for 90 days to 6 months, goals for 6 months to a year, and goals that are further down the road such as 10 years from now. I think one thing people get wrong is either they have no goals, or they have far too many goals at the same time.

Spread your goals out in small chunks so you can achieve incrementally, day by day. If your goal is to have your very own 757, though I believe is a great dream and goal to have, you may find yourself disappointed, even when you elevate yourself to the six figure status because you have not achieved the ultimate goal of owning that jet. By having such a large goal, and nothing in between, you're going to lose your focus and motivation.

Think of your goals as steps. If you want to get to the next floor of a building and there is no possible way to get there, how do you expect to ultimately reach the top floor? What's most likely going to happen is you will fall short of the end goal because you've lost focus with the aggravation getting from the ground floor to the next level, and to the next level after that. Build your steps to the top one by one.

Sometimes you will find that the path to your goals, or the plans to reach those goals may have to change. Look at is as having the same destination but taking an alternate route. Don't allow your goals to change, especially if by changing those goals, you are settling for less, or outright giving up. Because when you settle for a settled for life, you will not be nearly as happy as you have the potential to be. It's up to you and you alone.

There will be twists and turns in your journey, you'll likely even come close to falling off a cliff. When the obstacles, the twists and turns, and whatever else comes your way; keep your eyes focused on the goals you're going after. Only focus on the problem with a solution and not focusing on the problem to have something to complain about. That accomplishes nothing.

I heard a former New Orleans Saint's football player speak at a revival when I was a child. He told a story about some cotton, machine he used to work with growing up to pick cotton from the fields. He recalled how if even a small, stupid little piece of cotton got lodged incorrectly in the machine it wouldn't work correctly. He said you could get mad at it, yell and curse at it, take your shoes off and sit down in front of it. None of those options, however, would fix the problem, which was dislodging that small piece of cotton. It had to be done otherwise you were wasting your time. It's the same with your goals. You can't accomplish them by staying focused on the problem and offering no solution to move forward.

Take a moment and reflect on the following questions. I highly recommend writing the questions and answers down in your notebook.

What are your goals as an entrepreneur?

What are your financial goals?

What are your spiritual goals?

What other goals do you have?

How close are you to accomplishing one or all of

these?

What steps have you taken, or will take to make these goals a reality?

If and when you are faced with a challenge; how will you remain focused on your goals?

Chapter 11

Create Your Own Luck

"I believe that people make their own luck by great preparation and good strategy." Jack Canfield

What do you think of when it comes to luck? Is it the successful business men and women that have more money than they know what to do with, travel the world, and have influence? Do you think of luck as winning the lottery, receiving an unexpected check, or finding the right person at the right place and time?

Luck can mean different things to different people. The Oxford dictionary defines luck as; *"Success or failure apparently brought by chance rather than through one's own actions,"* or *"Chance considered as a force that causes good or bad things to happen."* You've heard the phrase just as I have when it comes to successful people, "oh they're just lucky." Maybe they are, then again maybe not. Have you ever thought that perhaps their luck was something they created themselves through hard work, tenancy, and persistence?

Winning the lottery may have some form of random luck, being successful in business and as an entrepreneur is a totally different animal. This form of luck if you will, is not something that happens randomly with no action, it's something one creates.

So how can you create good, more, and better luck for yourself? Here are five ways we can shape, or reshape our realities, and in turn create luck for yourself as an entrepreneur.

1. Connect with optimism

Idealistic individuals actually make a great deal of good luck, also known as good fortunes. There have been studies that have demonstrated that more than 80 percent of individuals who feel they're fortunate really work harder at making their good fortunes. On the other side, individuals who feel unfortunate have a tendency to trust that misfortune simply happens (to them, a ton) and that it isn't something they have any influence to change. Fortunate individuals see the world with optimism. At the point when awful things happen, and they do, it is their positive thinking that makes them stronger. They can lift themselves up and confront one more day, making all the better fortunes. So take advantage of your positive thinking and start making your own good fortunes.

This is a basic law of attraction. The seeds you are sowing, that shall you also reap in return.

2. Have an open mind, and be open to the possibilities

Become acquainted with the greatest number of individuals as you can and construct a broad system of contacts. Continually be on the look for potential open doors, and endeavor to get them going. Be interested in the conceivable outcomes, regardless of the possibility that it implies grasping an alternate state of mind about something, or a major change in your life or career.

By doing the same thing you've always been doing, you're not going to get different results. Keep your mind open, be open to the possibilities. You never know when the next great opportunity may present itself.

3. Trust your gut feelings

Very often, most individuals do not listen to their internal voice, their instinct, and after that soon think twice about it. How frequently have you said to yourself, "If I had just listened to myself?" whenever you need to make a decision on a critical choice about the future, clear your mind. Meditation is a great way to achieve this. By quieting your thoughts, you will have the capacity to hear your internal voice much better and follow up on it.

4. Shoot for the moon (and beyond)

Many of you have heard this before, "Shoot for the moon and you may very well catch some stars on your way down." Quite frankly it's very valid! You can make your own fortunes by setting objectives that you're not certain you can accomplish, and afterward pulling out all the stops and striving to make them genuine. By buckling down towards your greatest dreams, new, open doors can and will be acknowledged, including some you may never have considered. Grabbing these open doors and benefitting as much as possible from them is the manner by which we make our own good fortune.

5. There is no set finish line

"Go as far as you can see. When you get there, you'll be able to see farther." – Zig Ziglar

So as to keep on creating your own good fortune, you have to advise yourself that there is never really a finish line. One should never cease learning and developing. Advise yourself that there will never be a completion/finish line. Always continue learning, developing, and stay optimistic. By doing these things it will present to you the best fortunes of all, joy and happiness in your life and who you are.

The luck we have we are able to manifest into our own life. It's all in our mindset. Our thoughts become our reality. We make ourselves believe whatever it is we thing, regardless of how positive or negative those thoughts may be. Be mindful of the things you think, and what you feed into your mind.

If you want to change your luck, start with your thoughts. Over time you'll find a difference in what luck comes your way.

Chapter 12

Expect Failure

"Do not be embarrassed by your failures, learn from them and start again." –Richard Branson

Every successful person has experienced failure at one point or another. Most of us have the mindset of "failure is not an option," and also believe that failure is a bad thing. What most people don't realize is that we learn more from our mistakes and failures than we do from success. What shouldn't be an option is failing, tucking our tail between our legs, and never trying again.

Our own ego can be a stumbling block that won't allow us to learn from our mistakes and come back stronger in the next round. So many have failed either in the beginning, somewhere in the middle, or further down the road. Of all the people who have failed, only about 1% of these individuals become successful. Now why do you think that is?

I've been there; maybe you have too, or know

someone who has. Your company goes belly up, or you're unable to overcome the obstacles to even get your pursuit off the ground. It happens, just make sure to allow it to be a lesson on how to improve and do things differently. Do not allow failure to become a defeat to the point that you never dust yourself off and start again.

Thomas Edison said; *"I have not failed. I've just found 10,000 ways that won't work."*

Steve Jobs was ousted by the company he founded. Bill Gates' first company was an utter disaster. Milton Hershey started three different candy companies, only for each of them to fail. Arianna Huffington was rejected by 36 publishers. The list of successful people and their failures could go on for days, many who are well known, and just as many if not more, that are unknown. Again, failure happens. Expect it, embrace it, and learn from it.

What I'm not saying is to start a venture with the expectation of failure to the point that you do self-sabotaging things to yourself, or your business so it can fail. What I mean is, even when giving an honest 110%, failure may happen. Upon that failure, a great lesson can be learned when you look back and analyze what worked, what didn't work, what improvements can be made next time to ensure success, and to safeguard that previous mistakes won't be repeated.

If you have the attitude of "well, I failed again, but after 5 husbands, two bankruptcies, and four failed businesses, what else is new?" I highly doubt you will have a stellar comeback considering your self-defeating mindset. What you focus most on, you will in-turn attract back to you.

"Success consists of going from failure to failure without loss of enthusiasm." Winston Churchill

It's one thing to fail, it's another to never recover. Unfortunately, there are more people wanting you to fail than there are those wanting you to succeed. Your failure should not be your defining moment, your comeback, however, should be.

Chapter 13

Persistence

"Flaming enthusiasm, backed up by horse sense and persistence, is the quality that most frequently makes for success." Dale Carnegie

Persistence, one ingredient you cannot do without on your journey to achieving success as an entrepreneur. We hear a lot about persistence, especially from successful people. So what is persistence anyway?

The definition of persistence according to the Merriam-Webster dictionary is;
"The quality that allows someone to continue doing something or trying to do something even though it is difficult or opposed by other people."

Does this make sense to you? You see, persistence is what is needed to tune out the naysayers in your life. Persistence, along with a vision, goals, a positive mindset, and enthusiasm will guide you to your own pathway to success.

Most of the overnight success stories you read or hear about usually aren't usually so overnight. The people involved were persistent in their pursuit for quite some time, learned from their mistakes, but never stopped working towards their goals.

Things may not go as planned; you may find yourself in a situation where everything is against you. There may be times you want to throw your hands up, quit, and just go the normal and easy route. Sure, go ahead, knock yourself out. I've been there, you may have been there, or find yourself there somewhere in the future. Keep in mind, however, you are a champion. Champions do not quit, they are persistent!

"Make sure your worst enemy doesn't live between your own two ears." Laird Hamilton

One only truly fails if they do not learn from their mistakes and simply gives up because it's too hard. Everyone would be business tycoons and billionaires if it were easy. No one said it would be easy, however; anyone who tells you it's not worth it has long given up on their dreams and goals.

In this microwave society we live in, most of us

expect massive success almost instantly with as little work as possible involved. That's one reason so many people fail in network marketing, or any other entrepreneurial pursuit.

Okay, so you can't get "a *small* loan of a million dollars" to get started. And? Your point is? Remember the earlier story of Todd Graves? That man was persistent and stopped at nothing to get his first restaurant started, even after numerous bankers gave him a no, and highly recommended the easy way out. (Getting a "real" job). It gets better. Mr. Graves started out working 20 hours a week when he finally did get his first restaurant opened. Would you be willing to make that much of a sacrifice?

Folks, let me tell you, persistence pays off. You've got to keep at it. Keep making those phone calls. Keep setting appointments. Continue handing out your business cards. Do not take no for an answer. If someone says no, find someone who will say yes. If no one says yes, then do whatever it takes to make your dream, goal, pursuit, whatever it is a reality. Do not quit. Keep striking even if you're tired, you don't want to, and when you find yourself losing all hope. Keep going, give your very best.

"Nothing in this world can take the place of persistence. Talent will not: nothing is more common than unsuccessful men with talent. Genius will not; unrewarded genius is almost a proverb. Education will not: the world is full of educated derelicts. Persistence and determination alone are omnipotent."
Calvin Coolidge

Chapter 14

Get off your rear and do something already

"Inaction breeds doubt and fear. Action breeds confidence and courage. If you want to conquer fear, do not sit home and think about it. Go out and get busy." – Dale Carnegie

You can do all the rah rah seminars, listen to audio, read books, think positive, and talk a good game. If you're not actually willing to get off the sofa, turn off the television and other distractions; you're doing a whole lot of nothing, and going nowhere fast. Now some of you have decided to get off the sofa, but now what? What are you supposed to do now? Let's face it, owning a business is great because you don't have anyone telling you what to do. What sucks about owning a business is you do not have anyone telling you what to do.

Here are a few basic starter tips to start attracting customers, clients, and prospective business partners.

These tips include, but are not limited to:

1. Harness the power of the internet
- Advertise through social media
    - Create a business page on Facebook, Twitter, and Instagram

        - (HASHTAGS ARE YOUR FRIEND) # # #

        - Be mindful of your sales & marketing tactics, you do not want to come across as spammy or have yourself placed in "Facebook jail" because you bugged the crap out of all of your 300 "friends" on Facebook about your new pursuit. (I mention because I've seen it happen.)

- Post ads on sites such as craigslist and Angie's list
  - o Do not put all your eggs in one basket when it comes to marketing your business online, use every available free resource you can find

- Create an online presence with videos online with sites such as YouTube

Use the internet as a tool to attract customers, clients, and prospective business partners that are far more targeted than calling everyone you know and giving flyers strangers.
Here are a few questions you need to think about when finding your target audience:

A. What problems do they have that I can help solve?
B. If they have questions; what questions can I answer?
C. How can I be relatable to them?
D. What is unique about the product or service I offer?

2. Get physical marketing materials
- At the very least get some business cards (but don't go hog wild on your advertising budget just yet)

- If you opt to use other marketing materials such as signs, postcards, pens, coffee mugs, flyers, ect. Start small, regardless of how much you have available to spend. Remember, we do things differently now than we did in the past. If you tap into the internet, and build a presence, you probably will not need very much physical marketing materials.

3. Start talking to people

- It's inevitable at some point you are going to have to start talking to people to grow your business

- Get comfortable with what you have to say, make it flow naturally in conversation, and avoid sounding like a pushy sales person (let's face it, no one likes a pushy sales person, regardless if these people are in your warm or cold market. Remember, not everyone is in your target market.)

- Overcome your fear (if applicable), of speaking to people about your business and what you can do to make their life easier, convenient, provide them peace of mind ect. (Talk up the benefits of what you offer and what's in it for them, talk less about the features.)

- Don't hound your friends and family for their business. If you do, you'll find yourself having your calls and texts ignored. You will also find your family isn't all that thrilled to see you at gatherings when all you have to say is something about your business and why you should join them. (Trust me, I know)

- Reach out to other entrepreneurs in the same industry as well as industries unrelated. You need to expand your market.

4. Start reading, start learning, start applying the newfound knowledge

- The only way to be successful is to fill your mind with knowledge. Start reading books about business, self-help & self-improvement, other entrepreneurs, money, the industry you're in, current market trends, the products & services you offer, ect. You should be filling your mind with usable knowledge more than watching TV and playing games.

- I highly recommend reading:
    o Sleeping Giant No More – (by yours truly)
    o Think and Grow Rich – Napoleon Hill
    o You are a badass – Jen Sincero (abet PG-13 due to language, but still a fantastic read and one of my all-time favorites)

These are a few books I would highly recommend reading after completing this one. Also sign up for email communication, recommending great books to read. Tai Lopez has a free mailing list you can join. He frequently sends out information about books he has read or currently reading, that can help you as you climb your way to the top.

The examples in this chapter are just scratching the surface, I understand that. What is truly important is your desire for change, and how close you are to making a decision to start or expand your business.

So if you have not done so already, get off the sofa and start taking action. The longer you wait, the longer it will be to yield results from your efforts.

Chapter 15

Piecing it all together

"Great things are done by a series of small things brought together." Vincent Van Gogh

Here are a few things you can do starting right now to make change occur in your life and assist you in your climb to the top.

1. Follow your passions

Some say that following your passions is bad advice. For every article stating that following your passions is bad advice, you can find that many more saying the opposite.

This is a situation honestly, where you have to find what's right for you. Many of us are programed to seek acceptance from others, and for someone to tell us what to do, instead of figuring out what works for us individually.

If organic gardening is your passion, by all means find a way to make it profitable for you. We live in a day in age where we have a nearly limitless amount of opportunity to make a life for ourselves that is fulfilling, fun, and rewarding to our overall well-being.

You could take your knowledge about gardening and post videos online, write a book, start a blog, and set up a Facebook page teaching others techniques for growing the perfect tomato, or how to compost.

If inputting formulas and calculations in a spreadsheet isn't your passion, why on earth are you doing it? It may be a steady job with a steady income, but is that something that brings fulfillment to your life?

If what you're doing isn't fulfilling your life, use it as a stepping stone to propel you towards where you want to be and what you're passionate about.

2. Meditate

Meditation can provide a wealth of benefits. It's a great way to relieve stress, assist you with problem solving, allows you to face your fears, and become a better business person to name a few.

It may be difficult starting out, especially if you've never done any form of meditation before. I highly recommend using a self-guided meditation that you can easily find online. Personally, I've had some great meditation experiences and some that were not so great either. So don't get too upset if you find your mind wandering, or unable to stay in a meditative state for very long.

I remember one session where I was completely in the zone, moments later I opened my eyes only to be disappointed that I was no longer in the meditative state. My point is it's okay, because it took just a moment to get back where I needed to be.

Reflection and meditation can transform you into a more compelling businessperson. It gives you an edge when you are managing other individuals, whether they are representatives, accomplices, or contenders.
As an entrepreneur who meditates, you can figure out how to be quiet and responsive, rather than fatigued and reactive to issues. You will have a superior comprehension of yourself and your feelings, and, hence, will have the capacity to oversee them further bolstering your good fortune.

You additionally figure out how to improve as an audience and be more mindful of what is circumventing you. This gives you an edge in transactions and negotiations.

3. Exercise

General exercise activity can have a significantly positive effect on anxiety, depression, and other mental issues. It likewise soothes stress, enhances memory, helps you rest better, and supports general mind-set. Furthermore, you don't need to be a wellness fan to profit from exercise or spend hours at the gym. Even a brisk walk a few days a week, or other physical activities can go a long way.

"A life without exercise is, simply, a life without vigor. Exercise doesn't mean hours at the gym, sweating and working until every muscle in your body is sore, but it does mean sometimes making a decision to let other things go for an hour or two so that you can take care of one of the most important elements of your life on this planet: your body." Tom Walsh

4. Eat healthier

I am just as guilty as the next person when it comes to indulging in foods that are not so healthy. The issue at hand is the foods we eat in many cases are substances that resemble food and are full of ingredients that can and do affect our health and thought process.

5. Cut back on mental junk food

Just as we should be mindful of the things we put into our body; we should be mindful of the things we feed into our mind. Unless the tv show, magazine, online resources, or news isn't going to help you fulfill your goals and dreams; practice extreme moderation with the mindless mental junk food. A decade from now, will it really matter what happened on that soap opera today, or what the Kardashians are up to?

6. Use technology as a tool, not a distraction

Technology can be the greatest tool to unleash your inner entrepreneur and to assist you as you climb your way to the top. That being said, however, technology can be the biggest distraction. Sadly, most people allow technology to serve as a distractor and not a tool for success.

Limit your time for social media, games, apps, ect. If you are not using social media to grow your business, limit your time reading posts that are irrelevant to your goals or playing games that add no value to your life.

7. Read More

There are many benefits of reading on a daily basis. To help your growth personally and in your business; reading is essential.

Some of the benefits include, but are not limited to:
- Expanded knowledge
- Reduction of stress
- Improved focus and concentration
- Mental stimulation
- Expansion of your vocabulary
- Improved memory

Warren Buffett's secret is reading 500 pages per day. By reading more you earn compound knowledge.

You may not have the stamina to read a book per day, much less a book per week. I get it, and that is perfectly fine. Make a commitment to take 15 to 30 minutes out of your daily routine and dedicate to reading a book or article that will pay you the dividends of knowledge. Disconnect from distractions and dedicate that time allotment for your own personal growth.

As time progresses, you will build the focus and stamina to read more that will allow you to further expand your knowledge. The more you do something the easier it becomes. The more you focus on reading, the easier it will be to absorb the information.

8. Find a mentor

A life coach or business mentors are a great option and can be a significant asset to entrepreneur should take advantage of. Starting a business honestly should never be a terrifying or overwhelming experience, filled with questions, fear, or doubt. It ought to be a community oriented ordeal amassing the learnings of the several entrepreneurs who have officially assembled fruitful organizations, and can help you move more quickly and maintain a strategic distance from known pitfalls in light of their years of experience, as business people themselves.

These coaches or business mentors all come from different walks of life, each of them share experiences that can help you deal with areas where you might be having an issue. Along these lines, seek out the guides who are masters of your particular industry, or your particular business issue, on a case-by-case premise. This isn't the same as finding a long-term person that would serve on your team. These would be those people that have been where you have been, and an ear to listen as you make your way through the different stages of your business. As you and your business grow, you will find new people along the way that you can seek guidance from that will help you in your climb to the top.

9. Surround yourself with like-minded people

Similar to seeking out a mentor; you must also surround yourself with other people that are entrepreneurs themselves. These people will understand your why a lot easier than someone that is full of the employee mindset.

Although these people may not be in the same niche or industry as you, there are many good things that can come from a relationship with other fellow entrepreneurs. Not only could there be the potential to provide services to each other, it can also lead to expanding your network and prospects.

You have the opportunity to share ideas and best practices from your pursuit and learn what worked for them as well.

We have the opportunity to expand beyond local entrepreneurs; we can easily reach out to and build a relationship with people across the state, country and world. Use this to your advantage.

Final thoughts

Remember the first few questions you were asked to write down? Let's look them over, shall we?

What are you doing currently?

What do you want to do?

Are you happy with how things are going right now in your life?

What are your aspirations?

Where do you see yourself in a month, six months, a year, five years, ten years from now?

If you have not written down these questions with their answers, do so now. You need to put in writing where you are and where you want to go. Review these questions and answers frequently, adjust them as needed.

To make a change happen in your life, and in your business, you've got to do things differently. Keep this in mind on those days when you find yourself creeping back to the sofa to binge watch a season of your favorite show instead of reading or building your business. You are where you are because of the decisions you've made. If you want to go somewhere else, you've got to take a different route. The same efforts will not yield different results.

Conclusion

"There is no real ending. It's just the place where you stop the story." -Frank Herbert

Before closing out this book, I'd like to share a few final thoughts and quotes to sum up a few of the things we discussed throughout the chapters.

As you climb to the top and as you unleash the power of your inner entrepreneur, remember the stories and principles you encountered throughout the book. It's up to you and only you to get the fire lit under your rear end and take action. Only when you make the decision, and not want to, want to do something, will you find yourself taking action despite any obstacles.

Each day is a blessing we are each gifted with. Do not squander your time with trivial mindlessness. Make a commitment to read more, watching TV less, and expand your knowledge daily. By filling your mind with knowledge instead of mental junk food, you will not only reap the benefits that reading provides, but it also will provide you with the tools, ideas, and principles that will help you continually grow.

As you learn, and the more you learn; share your knowledge with others. Share what you know with people who are willing to listen, have the desire to expand their knowledge, and are eager to conquer their pursuit, whatever that pursuit may be.

Road blocks, pot holes, and sudden turns will come throughout your path. As time progresses, and the more you learn, the easier it will be to learn the signs of upcoming roadblocks, and how to overcome them. Face any challenges head on, have the courage to fight another day, and have the faith you will make it to your goals.

"A river cuts through rock, not because of its power, but because of its persistence."- Jim Watkins

Remain persistent in your pursuit. If one door is closed with a no, find another door. If you cannot find another door, build one. If you cannot build a door, find someone to build one for you. If you cannot find someone to build a door for you, bulldoze the wall down. If you have the will, the burning desire; find a way.

"Success is the sum of small efforts, repeated day in and day out." - Robert Collier

Finally, I will leave you with this. Success is not something you can achieve once, and then do nothing for the remainder of your days. You also cannot work only until you start seeing results, then sit back, relax, and believe you're on the path to smooth sailing to the top. It doesn't work that way. So do not think for a moment that the start of your results is your stopping point. It's merely an indication to continue pushing forward. Quite frankly, success is something that is rented, and your payment is due each and every day. What you sow today you will reap for harvest in the future. Keep sowing and keep growing.

"To succeed, you must have tremendous perseverance, tremendous will. 'I will drink the ocean,' says the persevering soul; 'at my will mountains will crumble up.' Have that sort of energy, that sort of will; work hard, and you will reach the goal." - Swami Vivekananda

Other books for your consideration:
Sleeping Giant No More: Wake up and see the greatness within you

Follow me on social media:
Twitter @curthinson

www.ingramcontent.com/pod-product-compliance
Lightning Source LLC
Chambersburg PA
CBHW060348190526
45169CB00002B/519